598   Porter, Keith
Por

      On the wing

THE ANIMAL KINGDOM

ON THE WING

KEITH PORTER

Editorial planning
Jollands Editions

SCHOOLHOUSE PRESS, Inc.

Photographic credits

t = top b = bottom l = left r = right

cover: Stephen Dalton/NHPA

4 Philip Shaw/NHPA; 5 ANT/NHPA; 12b Manfred Daneggar/
NHPA; 13b Peter Johnson/NHPA; 15 Philippa Scott/ NHPA;
16t Peter Castell/Aquila; 16b E. Hanumantha Rao/NHPA;
18t Stephen Dalton/NHPA; 18b M.F. Soper/NHPA; 19 Brian
Hawkes/NHPA; 20 Hellio & Van Ingen/NHPA; 21t Brian
Hawkes/NHPA; 22 Philippa Scott/NHPA; 23t Joe B. Blossom/
NHPA; 23b Brian Hawkes/NHPA; 24 Wayne Lankinen/Aquila;
25t Roger Tidman/NHPA; 25b Bryan Sage/Aquila;
27t M.C. Wilkes/Aquila; 27b N. Williams/Aquila; 28 Bryan
Sage/Aquila; 29t Stephen Krasemann/NHPA; 30t Peter
Johnson/NHPA; 30b J.J. Brookes/NHPA; 31 R.J. Erwin/NHPA;
32/33 Stephen Krasemann/NHPA; 32b Stephen Dalton/NHPA;
33 Haroldo Palo Jr/NHPA; 34 A.T. Moffett/Aquila;
35b R.J. Erwin/NHPA; 36 Philip Wayre/NHPA;
37t A. Sutherland/Aquila; 37b G.D.T./NHPA; 38 J. Jeffery/
NHPA; 39t R.W. Knightbridge/NHPA; 39b Brian
Hawkes/NHPA; 40 L. Campbell/NHPA; 41t Patrick
Fagot/NHPA; 41b L. Campebll/NHPA; 42 Aquila; 43, 44
M.F.Soper/NHPA; 45t James Hancock/Aquila

Note to the reader
In this book there are some words in the text which are printed in **bold** type. This shows that the
word is listed in the glossary on page 46. The glossary gives a brief explanation of words which may
be new to you.

Contents

Introduction   4

The First Birds   6

Thousands of Types   8

A Bird's Body   10

How Birds Fly   12

Dance and Courtship   14

Nests and Eggs   16

The Young Bird   18

The long journeys   20

The Polar Regions   22

Seabirds   24

Wetland Birds   26

Birds in the Open   28

Birds in Deserts   30

Birds in Rain Forests   32

Birds in Woodlands   34

The Northern Forests   36

Mountain Birds   38

City Life   40

Birds on Islands   42

Birds in Danger   44

Glossary   46

Index   48

Introduction

▼ Birds can live in almost every habitat on earth. This brown skua is one of the many types of bird which spend the summer in the Antarctic. The skua escapes from the very cold Antarctic winter by flying thousands of miles to warmer lands.

It is easy to tell birds from the other animals. Birds are the only group of animals to have **feathers**. All birds have two wings, instead of two arms, as well as two legs. Most birds are good fliers. A few types have lost the use of their wings and are either fast runners or strong swimmers. The swimmers use their "wings" as flippers.

Every bird has a bony **skeleton** with a **backbone**. Animals with backbones are called **vertebrates**. Other types of vertebrates are the **amphibians**, the **reptiles**, and the **mammals**.

Birds are a very successful group of animals. They live everywhere in the world, from the hostile deserts to the busiest cities.

Birds Across The World

One reason for the birds' success is their ability to fly. Birds can travel long distances over the oceans and the land, allowing them to move to warmer countries when the winter comes. Birds can also fly to safe places which other animals cannot reach, like the islands in the middle of the oceans.

The greatest numbers of birds live in the **tropical rain forests** where there is plenty of food. Other forest areas, the grasslands, the mountains, and the deserts are all home to different types of birds. Even the cold **polar regions** are home to many birds.

Some types of birds, like the penguins, live in only one place, or **habitat**. Others, like the crows, live in many habitats.

▼ Many types of bird have adjusted to life in one habitat. Parrots live in the warm tropical regions where their food is always available.

Warm Bodies

All animals need warmth to stay alive. Most animals depend on the sun to keep them warm. Birds and mammals are different. They can make heat inside their bodies, which means that they are **warm-blooded** animals.

Birds are also kept warm by their feathers. Next to their skin, they have soft, short feathers called **down**. The down feathers keep the heat in and the cold out. They can be fluffed up if the weather is really cold.

The First Birds

The first birds appeared about 150 million years ago, long before the first people. The world was a very different place then. It was full of plants and animals which are no longer found today. The skies were ruled by flying reptiles called the **pterosaurs** (*terror-sores*).

The first birds came from a group of early reptiles which died out many millions of years ago. From this ancient group of reptiles the **dinosaurs** and crocodiles developed. The dinosaurs died out 65 million years ago, the crocodiles are alive today. Although they look very different, the crocodiles are the nearest living relatives of the birds. Birds can be thought of as being reptiles with feathers.

▲ Archaeopteryx lived about 150 million years ago. The fossils of Archaeopteryx are important because they have shown scientists that birds came from reptiles.

▼ One of the earliest birds was Hesperornis. This bird could not fly, but it was a good swimmer. It lived near the sea and fed on fish.

Clues to the Past

How do we know about animals of the past? When animals die, sometimes their bodies sink into the mud. Over the years, their bodies become covered by layers of mud. Over millions of years, this mud is pressed into rock. The bones and teeth of the animals become part of the rock. These remains are called **fossils**.

Scientists can tell the age of the fossils from the rocks in which the fossils are found. The scientists may be able to reconstruct a skeleton of the animal. The skeleton can tell them how big the animal was, and if it walked, swam, or flew. The fossils of birds are rare because their small bodies were eaten by other animals.

▼ Ichthyornis is also known as "the fish bird." It was a seabird and led a life similar to the gulls and terns of today. Ichthyornis measured about eight inches.

Towards True Flight

The fossil of an early bird-like animal was found in a quarry in Germany in 1861. This animal was named Archaeopteryx (*ark-e-op-terr-ix*). The skeleton looked like that of a small lizard. It had teeth, a long bony tail, and wings with claws. The wings showed clear signs of having had feathers. This made Archaeopteryx very different from other reptiles of that time because they did not have feathers.

Scientists think that the **ancestors** of Archaeopteryx were tree-lizards, which leaped from tree to tree. Their clawed "arms" helped them to grip on to the tree trunks. These reptiles gradually learned to **glide**. Archaeopteryx probably did not fly, but glided from tree to tree. It did not have a strong **breastbone** like birds do today. The breastbone is where the flight muscles are attached.

The first true flying birds developed about 90 million years ago. They included a small seabird called Ichthyornis (*ik-thee-or-nis*).

7

Thousands of Types

There are nearly 9,000 types of birds in the world today. Each type of bird has its own color pattern, or **plumage**. Each type of bird also has its own special food. This means that many kinds of birds can live side by side and not have to fight over the same food.

The largest birds are those which have lost the use of their wings. The ostrich can be over 7½ feet tall. The smallest birds are the hummingbirds. The fairy hummingbird of Cuba is just over 2 inches long and weighs about ⅒ of an ounce.

hummingbird

flamingo

As well as being very different in appearance, these birds all eat different foods. The largest bird, the ostrich, eats fruits, seeds, and leaves. The eagle is an expert hunter and feeds on small land animals. The flamingo feeds on tiny animals which it finds in shallow water. The kingfisher dives into rivers and lakes when it sees a fish. The woodpecker has a strong beak for digging insects out of trees. The tiny hummingbird feeds on the nectar from flowers.

bald eagle

blond-crested woodpecker

kingfisher

Birds in Groups

Birds are divided into groups. These groups show us how the birds are related to one another. The 9,000 types of birds are split into 28 groups called **orders**. Each order contains birds which are alike in shape or the way in which they live. One order, for example, contains all the **birds of prey**. This order includes eagles, hawks, falcons, and vultures. Other orders, such as the **perching birds**, contain thousands of different types. Some orders contain only one type of bird. The emu is in an order unto itself.

▶ All birds belong to one of 28 orders. Each order is divided into families. Each family is divided into individual types, or species.

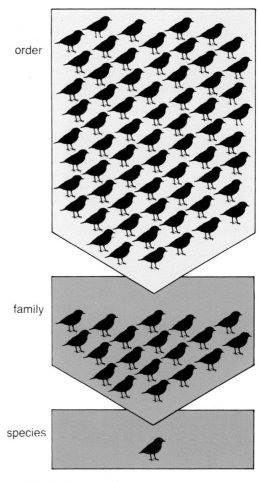

order

family

species

ostrich

A Family Likeness

Almost all of the orders are split into **families**. Some families include birds which look alike. For example, the four members of the flamingo family are exactly the same shape. They differ only in their size and their varying shades of pink color. This color variation is also true for the penguins, turkeys, kingfishers and many other bird families.

Most families include birds which have the same **habits**. This may mean that they live in the same place, like the woodpecker family which lives in the forests, or the gull family which lives near the ocean. It may also mean that the birds eat the same type of food. For example, all members of the hummingbird family drink **nectar**.

A Bird's Body

The bodies of birds are light and strong. Their skeletons have many hollow bones which reduce their weight. These bones are kept strong by tiny supports inside the bones.

Like many animals, birds have **lungs** for breathing. Unlike other animals, the birds also have balloons of air in their bodies called **air sacs**. The air sacs hold the air as it is breathed in. The air then passes to the lungs in a continual flow. This way, air moves through the lungs all the time and gives the birds as much **oxygen** as possible.

Bird Senses

All birds have good eyesight in order to see ahead when they are flying. Most birds use their eyes for hunting. The birds of prey have the keenest eyesight of all.

Many birds have very good hearing. Birds often use "songs" to talk to each other. Few birds have a good sense of smell or taste. Most find their food by its color or shape.

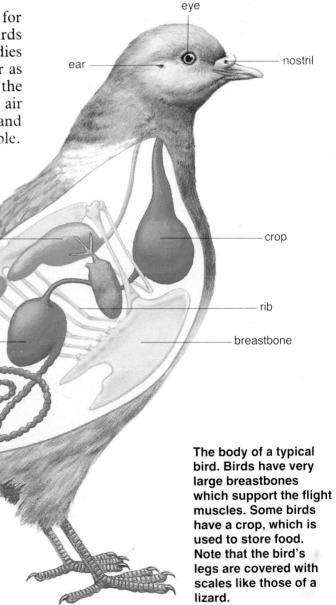

The body of a typical bird. Birds have very large breastbones which support the flight muscles. Some birds have a crop, which is used to store food. Note that the bird's legs are covered with scales like those of a lizard.

Beaks

A bird's beak is an important tool. Birds use their beaks to pick up things. Most birds use their beaks when they are building their nests to carry mud, sticks, or grass.

Most of the beak is made of bone. Around the bone there is a layer of hard material called **keratin**. The quills of a bird's feathers and our fingernails are also made of keratin.

Beaks come in all shapes and sizes. Different shapes are needed to feed on different foods. Long, thin beaks are used to probe into mud for worms. Strong, hooked beaks are used for tearing up food. The sharp beaks of the woodpeckers are used to bore into trees.

Feathers

Feathers are very important to birds. Feathers keep the heat in and the cold and water out. Besides being necessary for flight, they also provide **camouflage** on the ground. Each bird has several shapes of feathers. The broad, long feathers make up the wings. The shorter, fine feathers cover the outside of the body.

Birds **molt** at least once a year. The old feathers gradually drop out and are replaced by new ones. Birds spend a lot of time cleaning and oiling their feathers. This is called **preening**, and it is done by using the beak as a comb.

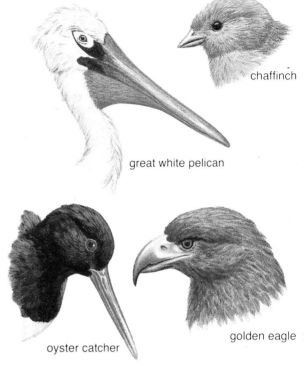

chaffinch

great white pelican

oyster catcher

golden eagle

▲ The beaks of these birds are shaped to eat different foods. The beak of the eagle tears up meat. The beak of the chaffinch crushes hard seeds. The pelican has a pouch for catching fish. The beak of the oyster catcher opens shells.

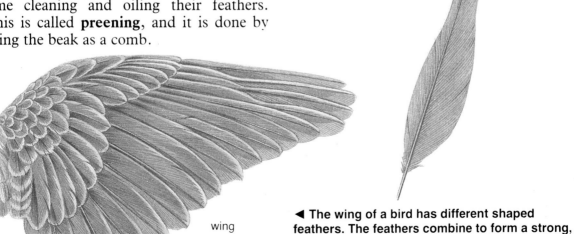

feather

wing

◀ The wing of a bird has different shaped feathers. The feathers combine to form a strong, light wing which keeps the bird in the air with the minimum of effort.

11

How Birds Fly

People have always wished that they could fly. We cannot fly because we do not have wings, and our bodies are too heavy. If we jump into the air, our strength gives us the **lift** to get us off the ground. It is our weight, however, which brings us down. Birds are light animals and have strong flight muscles which flap their wings. The lift that the wings produce overcomes their weight, so the birds can fly.

Wings and Wind

The shape of a bird's wing is very important. As it cuts through the air, the wing's shape helps to give the bird lift. The air passing over the top of the wing has further to go than the air passing beneath the wing. The result is that the air beneath pushes the wing upwards.

▲ The wing movements of a bird in flight.

The flapping of a bird's wing pushes it through the air in the same way that swimmers push their way through the water. The wings give the bird forward movement, or **thrust**. During flight, the bird's wings twist and turn. Attached to the breastbone is a large pair of muscles which pulls the wings down against the air. A smaller pair of muscles pulls the wings back over the body.

◄ A mute swan taking off. Swans need to build up speed before they can lift themselves up into the air.

When you ride a bicycle, you feel the wind in your hair. This is the pull, or the **drag**, of the air. If you crouch down into a smooth, compact shape, you will go faster. Look at a bird's shape in the air. It is smooth and **streamlined**. The bird's shape helps it to overcome the drag.

Riding on Air

Air rises when it is warm. Once a bird is in the air, it can make use of the rising warm air currents, called **thermals**. If the thermals are strong enough, they will lift a bird up high without it having to flap its wings. Some large birds, such as eagles and vultures, have wings which are shaped to take as much advantage as possible of the rising air. These birds are called **soaring birds**.

When a soaring bird has reached a great height, it can glide a long way without any effort. As it glides, it searches for another thermal to take it up high again.

▼ An albatross is a large, soaring bird. The long, thin wings are shaped so the albatross gets as much lift as possible from the strong sea breezes.

Dance and Courtship

Much of a bird's life is spent raising its young. Most birds produce young, or **breed**, at least once every year. Some birds raise many **broods** of young in their lifetimes. In order to produce young, a male and a female need to form a **pair**.

The first step towards the forming of a pair is when the male bird chooses a place to nest. Once a good place is found, the male sets up his **territory**. The territory is the area in which he will bring up his family. The male tells other birds where his territory is by singing.

A Fierce Display

The male birds often have to put on fierce dances, or **displays**, to maintain control of their territory. Many males ward off **intruders** with their loud songs. The strongest, most colorful and noisiest males get the best territory.

Birds usually avoid actual fighting. Each male soon learns where his neighbor's territory ends. Most types of birds have bushes, trees, or posts which they use as territorial markers, or signing points.

Different types of birds need different size territories. A large eagle needs many square miles to gather food for its young. A tiny wren needs only 50 square feet. The size of the territory depends upon how much food can be found, and how much each bird needs.

hawfinch

European robin

Adélie penguin

bird of paradise

▲ A selection of different courtship acts. The hawfinches rub beaks. The European robins offer each other food. The penguin performs a dance. The bird of paradise displays his plumage.

Courtship

If a female bird comes into the male's territory, the male will dance or display in front of her. This is called **courtship**. The male attracts the female in a variety of ways. Some males simply move their wings or their head. Other birds, like peacocks, use their colorful feathers to make beautiful displays. Some of the finest displays are made by the birds of paradise. Each male bird has a different shape and color pattern. The male birds use their colorful crests, frills, or long tails to attract the females.

The male frigate bird and the umbrella bird have unusual displays. They blow out red pouches which are on their necks. The females are attracted to the males with the biggest and brightest pouches.

Some pairs, like the grebes, dance together. Other birds offer each other pieces of food. These acts make sure that the pair stays together. Most pairs will stay together for one year. Some pairs will stay together for life.

▼ A male frigate bird displays its bright red pouch to a female.

Nests and Eggs

Nests are the places where birds bring up their families. The nests are built to protect the eggs and the young birds. Many animals like to eat eggs or young birds. To prevent this, most nests are built in places which are difficult for other animals to reach. Cliffs, trees, and burrows are all safe places for nests.

▼ The nest of a weaver bird hangs from a branch. The entrance tunnel is on the other side of the nest.

▲ The simple nest of a mallard duck hidden among some reeds. The nest is lined with soft feathers.

All Shapes and Sizes

Every type of bird has a different kind of nest. All nests must be big enough for the parent bird to sit on.

The simplest nests are platforms made of twigs or leaves. The insides of the nests are often lined with moss or feathers. More complex nests have "roofs." A nest with a "roof" is hollow and ball-like. The eggs are kept warm and dry inside.

The most complex nests are built by the weaver birds. These birds **weave** grass into a strong ball-shaped basket. Swallows and oven birds use mud to make their hard clay nests.

Some nests are well-protected. The nests of the broadbills and the sunbirds are hung from branches. Other birds make tiny entrances to their nests to prevent **predators** from reaching their young. The female hornbill seals herself inside a hollow tree until her eggs hatch. The male passes food to her through a tiny hole.

Birds' Eggs

A bird's egg is a tiny, enclosed world. The hard shell protects the growing bird inside. The shell is made from a kind of chalk. The egg white, or **albumen**, is a fluid which protects the **yolk**. The yolk is full of food. On the surface of the yolk is a tiny spot. This is the beginning of the new bird. The egg must be kept warm while the tiny bird grows inside. The parents must sit on the egg to keep it warm. This is called **incubation**.

Some birds lay up to 20 eggs in one nest. All the eggs are about the same size. The eggs which are laid on the ground are colored to match their surroundings, such as stones, gravel, or sand. The eggs which are laid in hidden nests can be white, yellow, or blue.

The birds which nest on cliffs, such as guillemots, have pointed eggs. These eggs are shaped to roll around in a circle preventing them from rolling over the edge of the cliff.

Birds' eggs come in many shapes and sizes, but they are all similar in other ways. Each egg has a hard shell, and it contains a yolk surrounded by albumen.

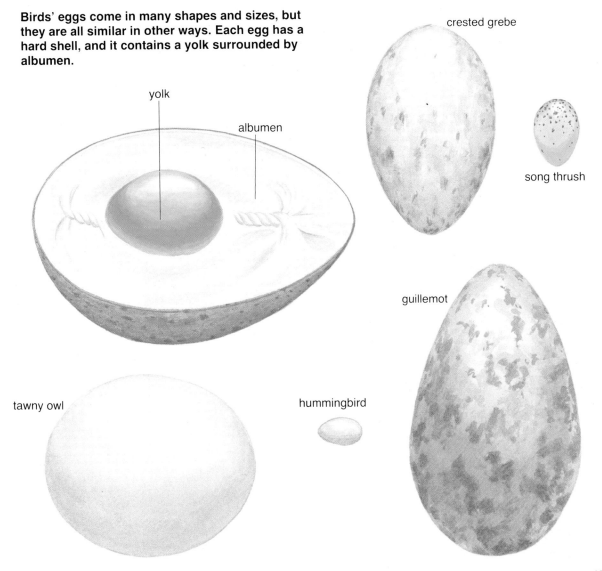

yolk

albumen

crested grebe

song thrush

guillemot

tawny owl

hummingbird

The Young Bird

When a young bird is ready to hatch, it must force its way into the world. Just before hatching, the young bird grows a hard bump on its beak called an egg tooth. The tiny bird uses the egg tooth to break through the eggshell.

Care of the Young

Young birds can be divided into two main types, **chicks** and **nestlings**. The chicks have fluffy bodies and can move about as soon as they hatch. For example, turkeys have chicks. The chicks stay close to their mother, following her wherever she goes. The mother leads them to food. Most chicks are patterned, or camouflaged, to match their surroundings. If the chicks are alarmed they stay still. This helps to protect them from their enemies.

▲ A blue tit feeding its nestlings. Their wide, gaping mouths demand food from their parents. The young blue tits stay in the nest for up to 21 days.

◄ An albatross lays a single egg which it incubates for two months. After hatching, the young bird is fed by the parents for a further nine months. This nestling is nearly ready to leave the nest.

The nestlings have to stay in the nest after hatching. An example of a nestling would be a baby robin. All the nestlings are blind, naked, and helpless when they hatch. They have to be fed by their parents. This is a non-stop job for the parent birds. Some smaller types of birds have to make up to 900 trips each day hunting for insects to feed their young. The birds of prey and seabirds only feed their young once or twice a day. They hunt for larger meals such as rabbits or fish.

The nestlings of small birds, such as tits or chickadees, stay in the nest for about 20 days. The nestlings of larger birds stay in the nest for much longer.

▼ An adult booby spreads its wings as an angry warning. The eggs would soon be stolen if they were left unguarded.

Leaving the Nest

After the nestlings leave the nest, they are called **fledglings**. The fledglings from one nest usually stay together. They still depend on their parents for food and protection. The cries of the young birds guide the parents to them at feeding time.

Some fledglings leave the nest before they can fly. This is a time of great danger. Many fledglings are eaten by predators. Some parent birds put themselves in danger by trying to lead an attacker away from their young. Other parent birds will strike out at an attacker.

The young bird is safer when it has learned to fly. Some young birds, like the swift, can fly on long journeys as soon as they leave the nest. Larger birds, like the California condor, can take many months to develop their flying skills.

The Long Journeys

Many types of birds breed in the far northern and southern parts of the world. The winters in these places are cold and harsh. During the winter, the insects, fruit, and other foods disappear. As the winter approaches, the birds fly on long journeys to warmer countries. In the spring the birds will return to their breeding grounds. This journey is called a **migration**.

Some birds fly very long distances when they migrate. Arctic terns fly all the way from the Arctic to the Antarctic, a journey of almost 11,000 miles!

Not all migrating birds, or **migrants**, leave because of the cold weather. Some birds from hot countries leave their homes as the summer approaches because all their food dries up and disappears in the hot, dry season.

Which Birds Migrate?

There are three main types of migrants. These are the summer visitors, the winter visitors, and the birds of passage.

The best-known summer visitors are the common, or barn, swallows. They breed all over northern America, Europe, and Asia. In the fall, the American swallows fly to South America. At the same time, the European swallows fly to central Africa. Other summer visitors to the northern countries include the bank swallows and the red-eyed vireos.

The winter visitors are the birds which breed in the Arctic. They include many types of geese, ducks, and wading birds. Snow geese and blue geese breed in the Canadian Arctic. In the fall, they fly south to the United States. Brant geese make a similar journey in Europe. They move south to feed along the warmer coasts.

Birds of passage are birds which are on the move. They can travel from the far north to the deep south. Each year, sanderlings and golden plovers pass over the United States. The common crane is a typical European bird of passage. It breeds in Scandinavia and winters in Africa.

▼ Cranes migrating south. Migrating birds often fly in a V-shaped formation. The leading birds create a "wake" of air which has a sucking effect. This allows the birds behind to fly with less effort.

Finding the Way

Some birds travel thousands of miles during their migrations. These birds always return to the same nest the next season. Scientists have tried to find out how the birds find their way. Many ideas have been suggested, but none give a full answer to the puzzle. Some birds follow the rivers or the coasts. Perhaps they learn the way. Many birds migrate at night. They cannot see the rivers or the land. **Experiments** have shown us that some birds find their way by using the stars as guideposts.

◀ A group of house martins gather before their long flight from northern Europe to Africa.

▼ The Arctic tern breeds in the far north of America and Europe. The birds fly to the southern tips of America and Africa when the winter comes. Some Arctic terns journey even further and reach Antarctica.

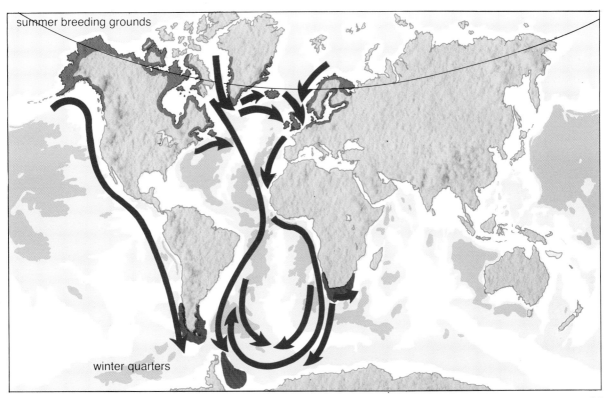

summer breeding grounds

winter quarters

21

The Polar Regions

Why do so many migrant birds breed in the Arctic and the Antarctic? Their long journeys are exhausting. Why don't they live in the warmer countries? The answer is that the cold polar regions are rich in food. During the short spring and summer, many plants and insects appear. The seas are full of tiny sea animals and fish.

Most birds of the polar regions have to leave as the winter approaches, and the land and the sea freeze over.

▼ A Dominican gull perches on an iceberg in Antarctica. The gull is a threat to other birds because it steals their eggs.

Antarctic Birds

Most of Antarctica is an icy wasteland. Nothing can live or grow on the snow and ice. Only the coasts offer food and shelter. The Antarctic birds all depend on the sea for food.

During the summer, the ice breaks up over the sea. The gulls and the petrels make their nests along the coasts. When the ice returns, they have to move north in search of the open sea.

Penguins are well-known Antarctic birds. The 16 types of penguins live along the cold southern shores. Their bodies are used to the cold. Under their skin is a thick layer of fat which helps to keep out the bitter cold. Penguins have lost the use of their wings. Their wings are used like flippers for swimming. Some penguins swim at speeds of 35 mph underwater.

The Emperor penguins are the only birds which can stay inland during the winter. These penguins breed during the winter. The male stands over the single egg keeping it warm beneath his body. He does not move for weeks at a time.

Arctic Birds

The northern portions of Canada, Greenland and Scandinavia are all part of the Arctic. Many birds live in the Arctic during the summer. In the winter, the land is bleak and frozen, but in the summer, the boggy land provides plenty of food.

Most birds arrive in the Arctic just as the snow melts. The birds must breed before the ice returns. Many types of geese, ducks and wading birds nest in the Arctic.

The seas of the Arctic are rich in food. Many types of gulls, skuas, and terns breed along the Arctic coasts. Birds called auks swim in the sea in search of food.

A few birds, like the willow grouse and the ptarmigan, remain on the edges of the Arctic all through the winter.

▲ Emperor penguins are the largest of the penguins. They stand three feet tall and weigh about 65 lbs.

▼ The snowy owl is an Arctic predator. It stays in the Arctic throughout the year. The snowy owl feeds on small mammals and birds.

Seabirds

The seas and oceans, which cover much of the earth, are rich in food. Birds which get their food from the sea are called seabirds. Most seabirds live along the coasts or on islands. A few seabirds can be found far from the land.

There are about 250 types of seabirds. The tropic birds, boobies, and frigate birds live in the warm tropical seas. The guillemots and razorbills live in the cold northern seas. The penguins and sheathbills are examples from the cold southern seas. Some types of seabirds such as the gulls, petrels, and terns, fly over all seas.

How are Seabirds Different?

A life at sea would not suit most land birds. They could not survive in the strong winds and waves. Seabirds have strong bodies and most of them are larger than the land birds. Seabirds have wings which are shaped to help them glide on the strong sea breezes. Some are long distance travelers. Each year, they fly from the northern seas to the southern seas.

The bodies of most seabirds are kept warm and dry by **waterproof** feathers. These feathers are kept well-oiled by preening. Some seabirds do not have waterproof feathers. They must dry themselves by spreading out their wings and "sunbathing." Birds that live in the cold seas have a layer of fat under their skin to help keep them warm.

Most seabirds can float on the sea. They swim by using their large **webbed feet** as paddles. Some seabirds can dive underwater in search of fish. Gannets and boobies dive like arrows from heights of 100 feet. They have very strong skulls to survive the shock of hitting the water from this height. Some diving seabirds have special "see-through" eyelids which help them to see underwater.

◄ **Cormorants are seabirds which dive into the sea to catch fish. They spread out their wings to dry them when they return to land.**

► **A noisy colony of gannets on the coast of New Zealand. The young birds have black and white speckled coats. They will fly 1,250 miles to the coast of Australia when they are fully grown. The parent birds will stay within a few hundred miles of the breeding site.**

Bird Colonies

All seabirds lay their eggs on land. Most seabirds breed every year. Seabirds often make their nests in large groups or **colonies**. Some colonies contain tens of thousands of birds. Gannets and guillemots often nest on the ledges of cliffs. Huge colonies of gulls and terns nest on gravel banks along the coasts. Other birds, like the albatrosses, nest together on remote islands.

Why do some seabirds nest in colonies? One reason is that many birds will gather where there is a good supply of food. Another reason is that living in a colony is safer since many animals, including birds, will eat eggs and young birds. The adult birds help each other to defend the colony. This makes it easier to protect the eggs and young birds from predators.

◀ A group of terns has spotted a shoal of fish. Each bird waits for a fish to come near to the surface. One bird has dived to grab a fish with its beak.

Wetland Birds

Streams, rivers, lakes, and **marshes** are all wetland areas. The wetlands are the home to many types of birds. These birds are found from the cold, boggy lands of the north to the hot, steamy swamps of the tropical lands.

Some wetland birds, such as ducks and grebes, are called swimmers. Others, such as herons, plovers, and sandpipers, are called **waders**. The waders are birds which feed in mud or shallow water.

Swimmers

Swimmers include geese, swans, ducks, grebes, and the divers. Altogether, there are about 175 types of swimmers. Most swimming birds are adapted for life on the water. Their feathers are waterproof. Most swimmers also have webbed feet which they use like paddles.

Geese, swans, and many types of ducks, eat plants. Some types of geese and swans nibble water plants. Others come ashore to **graze** like cattle. A few types, like the teal and mallard ducks, look for food in the mud. Other types of ducks use their bills to **filter** tiny plants and animals from the water.

Some types of ducks, grebes, and divers eat small fish, frogs, and insects. The black-throated diver, or Arctic loon, searches for its food underwater. Its smooth shape and large feet make it a good underwater swimmer. The canvasback duck and the tufted duck feed on plants and animals. They dive down to feed on the beds of rivers and lakes.

Waders and Others

There are over 400 types of wading birds. Some have long legs and necks. Others have thin beaks which probe into the mud for food. These birds, such as snipes and curlews, usually spend the winter along the coasts. In the summer, they breed on wet moorlands and marshes. They feed on small animals living deep in the mud or soil. Storks, herons, and cranes are other waders. They have long legs and strong, sharp beaks. They use their beaks to spear fish and frogs which they find in shallow lakes and rivers.

▼ Some wetland birds wade near the shore in search of food. The surface swimmers feed underwater. Other types swim deep below the surface. The non-swimmers grab prey which comes near.

kingfisher

heron

crested grebe

► A pair of mallard ducks. The male is the brightly colored one. Mallard ducks feed on small animals, plants, and seeds which are found in the mud or in shallow water.

▲ Flamingos are wading birds. They have a special way of feeding. A flamingo's tongue forces water through the bill. The bill catches the food particles and tiny animals which float in water.

ducks

There are 130 types of wetland birds which are neither swimmers nor waders. Dippers are small birds which live alongside fast-flowing mountain streams. They walk underwater along the beds of streams in search of water insects and small fish. The colorful kingfishers hunt from perches above rivers and streams. These birds catch fish by diving swiftly into the water.

Birds in the Open

Parts of the world are covered with large, grassy areas with few trees. These areas are called the grasslands. They include the **prairies** of North America and the **savannas** of Africa.

The open grasslands can be difficult places for birds to live. Most grasslands are dry and windy; it may not rain for months. Many grassland birds have to fly long distances in search of food and water. Trees are safe places for birds to build their nests, however there are few trees in the grasslands. Grassland birds have to nest on the ground. Predators, such as coyotes, foxes, and snakes like to eat the eggs and young birds.

Nests on the Ground

Many grassland birds have learned how to hide their eggs. Some, like the larks, build their nests inside clumps of grass. Others, like the grouse and prairie chickens, lay their eggs on the ground. Their nests are just small hollows, or **scrapes**, in the ground. The nests in the open contain dull, speckled eggs which are difficult to see. The eggs are well-protected when the mother is on the nest because her camouflaged plumage hides the eggs.

A few grassland birds build their nests in burrows. The burrowing owl uses the burrows of prairie dogs for its nest. Some ovenbirds use the burrows of mice or gophers. The red ovenbird builds a round, clay nest which is like a small fort.

▼ A well-camouflaged willow grouse sits quietly on her nest. The willow grouse grows white feathers in the winter to blend in with the snow.

Large Running Birds

The largest birds in the world live in the grasslands. These include the ostrich, the emu, and the rhea. The ostrich lives in Africa. It grows to over 8 feet in height and can run at a speed of 35 mph. The emu lives in Australia. The two types of rheas live in South America. Rheas are endangered birds. Many have been killed by farmers whose crops were eaten by the rheas.

All these birds have lost the use of their wings over millions of years. They no longer need to fly from their enemies. Instead, they have long, strong legs for running. Their speed, size, good eyesight, and sharp beaks help to protect them.

Ostriches, emus, and rheas all make their nests by scraping out holes in the ground. Male ostriches and rheas often look after their young forming "herds" of the young from several nests. The emus usually nest alone.

▲ A burrowing owl stands near to its nest in a prairie dog's tunnel. It keeps a sharp eye out for its prey, such as mice or lizards.

▼ A comparison, to scale, of the rhea, emu, and ostrich. They are all grassland birds. Although these birds look alike, they do not belong to the same family.

ostrich

emu

rhea

Birds in Deserts

Deserts are very dry places. During the day, they can be very hot, but at night they can be bitterly cold. These changes from hot to cold and the lack of water make the deserts very difficult places in which to live. Despite the difficulties, some types of birds only live in deserts. Most desert birds are light in color, helping to camouflage them.

Desert birds need to keep cool. The roadrunners and the coursers have long legs to help them keep their bodies off the very hot ground. The air is much cooler just above the surface. Most desert birds cannot stand the great heat and have to rest in the shade in the middle of the day.

▲ Water holes can be dangerous places. Because predators wait nearby, other animals drink as quickly as possible. Some of the flock keep watch while the other birds drink.

▼ A male sand grouse collecting water for his family. The water is carried in his belly feathers.

▶ Mourning doves are well suited to a life in hot, dry regions. They can survive without water much longer than most birds. This mourning dove has made its nest in a cactus.

The Need for Water

All plants and animals need water to stay alive. Some desert animals have bodies which can go without water for many days. Most desert birds, however, need water every day. Desert birds have one great advantage over the other desert animals. The birds can fly a long way to reach water.

The sand grouse can fly up to 55 miles each day in search of water holes. There are 16 types of sand grouse. Some drink only at night while others travel to the water holes in the mornings or the evenings.

The male sand grouse has a clever way of bringing water to its young. It uses its belly feathers like a bath sponge. After drinking, the male sits in the water to fill his "sponge." Then, he flies back to the nest where the chicks can drink the water which the sand grouse has soaked up in his belly feathers.

Some small birds, like finches, get enough water from the plants which they eat. They do not have to fly to get water from far away.

Feeding and Breeding

Birds need plenty of food and water when they are nesting. Most desert birds feed on plants or insects. In the desert, the plants and insects are only plentiful when there has been rain. These birds must breed when the rains come. It is only then that they can gather enough food and water for themselves and their young. Some birds, therefore, can only nest once every few years. Other desert birds, like the roadrunner, eat lizards and snakes. These birds do not have to wait for the rain before they gather enough food to breed.

Mourning doves feed their young with "pigeon milk." This is a very rich food which is mixed in the throat, or **crop**, of the adult birds. The dove chicks grow very quickly on this food.

The eggs and the young need to be protected from the hot sun. Small birds, like the desert wheatears, nest in burrows or crevices to escape from the sun. Other birds, such as the coursers and pratincoles, stand over their eggs to shade them. The Egyptian plovers cool their eggs and chicks with water.

Birds in Rain Forests

Forests in the hot, steamy parts of the earth, close to the **Equator**, are called tropical rain forests. These forests contain over half of all types of birds in the world.

Tropical rain forests can be divided into three main layers. Each layer of a rain forest contains many places for animals to live. The forest floor is dark, damp, and warm. It is thick with bushes and tree trunks. The middle layer includes climbing creepers and small trees. Above this layer, giant trees form a roof of branches, or a **canopy**, over the forest.

The Forest Floor

The birds which live on the forest floor usually have strong, pointed beaks and short, broad wings. Many forest floor birds hop or run along the ground. It is difficult to fly among all the tree trunks. Some birds find their food on the forest floor. The colorful pittas, or ground thrushes, for example, hunt for insects, and snails.

Some birds, like the cotingas, lyrebirds, and peacocks, fly down to small clearings in the forest floor for **courtship dances**. These dances attract the females. Some cotingas, like the male cock-of-the-rock, are very brightly colored.

The male bower birds build "tunnels" of sticks to attract the females. The males decorate their tunnels with colored feathers, stones, and flowers.

▶ A male cock-of-the-rock perching close to his display ground. If a female comes near, the male will fly down to the forest floor and try to attract her by performing a dance.

▲ Rainbow lorikeets wander through Australian forests in search of food. They feed on the nectar from flowers and on insects. Lorikeets belong to the parrot family.

▲ A toucan eating fruit in the treetops of a South American forest.

Above the Ground

The middle layer of the forest, between the ground and the treetops, is full of birds. There the birds feed on many insects, fruits, and leaves. Large flocks of birds wander in search of food. Each flock may contain a mixture of birds. They feel safer in large numbers. The fruit and seed eaters include the barbets, birds of paradise, and the parrots. The insect eaters include the motmots, broadbills, and manakins.

One of the finest groups are the American hummingbirds. They feed mainly on the nectar from flowers but will sometimes also eat a few insects.

Above the Trees

The birds which live in the forest canopy include the tanagers, the toucans, hornbills and some cotingas. The hornbills and the toucans have long colorful beaks. They use their beaks to reach the fruit on the thinnest of branches. Many of these birds spend their entire lives in the canopy.

Birds of prey also live in the canopy. The harpy eagle and the Philippine monkey eagle eat monkeys and other small animals.

Birds in Woodlands

▼ Members of the finch family are found in many parts of the world. The hawfinch is a small shy bird which often lives unnoticed in the trees. Its strong beak can break open the hardest seeds. The hawfinch lives in European woodlands.

Many parts of the world contain forests called woodlands. These forests have all four **seasons**. The woodlands are green, warm places in the spring and summer when there are many insects, buds, and seeds for the birds to eat. In the spring, the woodlands echo with the songs of the birds. This is the time when the male birds set up their territories. Each male sings to ward off any intruders and to attract a mate. The woodland trees lose their leaves each fall. By the time winter arrives, the woodlands are bare and cold and food for the birds becomes scarce.

Finding Food

Some woodland birds avoid the winter by migrating. These include the flycatchers and the warblers which eat only insects. The migrant birds leave the woodlands in the fall and fly to warmer countries in search of insects.

Other woodland birds stop eating insects in the fall. Instead, they feed on nuts, fruits, and seeds during the winter. The larger woodland birds are often predators. The predators survive all the year around by feeding on other birds and small mammals, such as mice.

Three kinds of woodland birds.

bullfinch

magpie

flycatcher

Bud and Seed Eaters

Birds of the finch family eat buds and seeds. Each type of finch has a different-shaped beak. The hawfinches have short, stout beaks with which they can crack open hard seeds. The goldfinches have beaks like tweezers. They pick the seeds from flowers. The chaffinches have small pointed beaks and eat small seeds. The bullfinches have short, round beaks and like to eat the new leaf buds.

▶ Acorn woodpeckers live in groups. They work together to gather acorns and care for the young.

Insect Eaters and Others

Many woodland birds eat insects. The tree creepers use their sharp beaks to pick the insects from the tree **bark**. The flycatchers, the vireos, and the warblers eat the insects from the leaves of bushes and trees.

The woodpeckers are among the largest insect eaters. They have sharp beaks which cut into trees in search of insect **grubs** or larvae. Woodpeckers have very strong heads, which can withstand the shock of the hammering. They also have very long tongues with sticky tips. Some types of woodpecker use their sticky tongues to catch ants deep in the ants nests.

Some types of birds, like magpies, jays, and crows, store nuts for the winter. The American acorn woodpecker stores acorns in tree trunks. Several birds may use the same tree. They guard the tree from other birds. Other birds hide insects and small animals. Birds gather a supply of food when it is plentiful in the summer and fall months.

The Northern Forests

The northern forests stretch across the far north of America, Europe, and Asia. These forests are called **coniferous forests**. The trees, which include pines, firs, and spruces, keep their needle-like leaves throughout the year. These trees are sometimes called evergreens.

Winters in the northern forests are very long and cold. Since forest birds can only breed in the short summers, many of the birds are only summer visitors. They fly to the forests to breed and return south to the warmer lands in the fall. A small number of birds manage to live in the northern forests all year around.

Surviving the Winter

The northern forests provide the birds with little food during the harsh winter. Much of the ground is frozen solid and covered with snow. Most birds of the northern forests, like the nutcrackers, eat seeds, nuts, and leaves. Some, like the crossbills, prefer one kind of food. Each type of crossbill eats only the seeds from one kind of tree.

Some birds move to the forests for shelter in the winter. Grouse and capercaillies move from the open, snow-covered plains to the forests. They survive by eating the leaves of the conifers. Few other birds are able to eat these leaves.

The birds must keep warm or they will die of cold in the winter. The feathers of the northern birds are often very fluffy. The grouse have more feathers than other birds. The extra feathers help to keep the warmth in and the cold out.

Owls and Hawks

The northern forests are home to many small mammals, such as the voles, shrews, hares, and lemmings. These animals are eaten by the birds of prey. Eagles, hawks, falcons, and owls are included in the birds of prey.

▲ The common crossbill feeds mainly on the seeds of spruce trees. Other crossbills eat the seeds of the larch and pine trees.

Birds of prey have very good eyesight and can see the tiniest movement of any animal. The buzzards and goshawks catch small mammals and birds while the peregrine falcons and sparrow hawks catch mainly birds.

Many of the small animals come out at night to feed. They are hunted by the northern owls which include the snowy owls, horned owls, and eagle owls. Owls have very good hearing as well as good eyesight. They use both these senses to hunt their prey. These birds are large enough to catch foxes.

In the summer, most birds of prey move further north to nest. Many other birds of prey fly into the northern forests from the warmer countries. They usually build their nests high up in the trees.

▼ A male capercaillie defends his territory by crying out an angry warning to other males which might be nearby.

▲ Peregrine falcons kill birds in mid air by diving on them at great speed. Their prey include pigeons, ducks, and grouse.

Mountain Birds

Mountains are bare, rocky places. Many mountain tops are covered with snow and ice. Strong winds blow, and the air is thin. Few types of birds can live on the mountains. The high winds, the cold, and a lack of food keep many birds away.

The birds that do live on mountains are either birds of prey or small perching birds. The birds of prey are strong enough to fly in the high winds. They survive by eating other animals. The small perching birds avoid the wind and live by clinging on to the mountains.

Hunters and Scavengers

The mountain birds of prey include hunters and **scavengers**, which are birds that feed on dead animals. The hunters, such as the eagles, kill small animals. They kill by using their clawed feet, or **talons**. The golden eagle dives on to its prey at speeds of up to 55 mph.

The vultures and the condors are the largest scavengers. They may feed away from the mountains. Both vultures and condors make good use of the wind; they can soar and glide over long distances. Some types can **soar** to over 24,000 feet. The bearded vulture, or lammergeier, is an unusual scavenger. It has learned to feed on the inner part, or **marrow**, of large bones. The bird drops the bones from the air to break them open.

◄ Eagles normally lay between two and four eggs. This is a golden eagle family. The young need plenty of food. The adult males do most of the hunting. They fly many miles in search of prey. The golden eagle kills animals as large as rabbits.

▲ A lammergeier soars high up in the sky. Lammergeiers spend much of their time searching for dead animals. Lammergeiers are not killers.

▼ Long toes help the wall creeper cling to steep rock faces. Wall creepers make their nests on small ledges. The young stay in the nests until they are nearly fully grown.

Perching Birds

The mountains have a winter and a summer like other places, or habitats. In the summer, the rocky ledges and the mountain slopes are covered with flowers. Some small birds feed on the insects and seeds found among these plants. In the winter, however, many of the smaller birds move further down the mountains.

The small birds survive on the mountains because they stay close to the ground. They would be blown away by the strong winds if they tried to fly very high off the ground.

The choughs (*chufs*) and the wall creepers have **adapted** to life on the mountains. Both types of birds search for insects on the rocky **crags**. The wall creepers can walk up or down the rocky cliffs.

City Life

Birds live wherever they can find food. Many birds live in our towns and cities, where there is plenty of food. The houses, roads, stores, and factories have driven most of the other animals away. Birds have learned to live in the most difficult surroundings. They can fly above the dangerous traffic, perch on buildings and telephone wires, and also build nests on buildings.

Nesting Sites

City and town birds have two types of nesting sites. Some, like the thrushes, use the green parts of the cities. They nest in the bushes and trees in the backyards and parks. Others, such as sparrows, pigeons, and starlings, nest on the outside of the buildings. They have learned to change their habits to suit their surroundings.

The birds which nest on the buildings treat them like cliffs. The window ledges of tall buildings are sometimes used by gulls and falcons. Starlings nest on the roofs of the buildings using the roofs in the same way as other birds use trees.

Swallows, swifts, and martins are used to making their homes in buildings. These birds build their mud nests under the **eaves** of the roofs. The chimney swift lives a dangerous life. As its name would indicate, it makes its nest inside a chimney. Luckily, this bird breeds in the summer when most chimneys are not in use. This swift nests inside hollow trees in the country.

▼ Pigeons are distantly related to the rock dove which nests on cliffs. Tall buildings in cities provide similar nest sites for pigeons.

Different Food

Sparrows and pigeons eat seeds and leaves in the country. Swallows and swifts catch flying insects. Starlings eat both plants and insects. Falcons eat small animals. These birds cannot find much food like this in the cities.

The city birds have to eat different kinds of food. Many survive on the scraps of food that we throw away. Birds pick through our garbage for food. Food is scarce for all birds during the winter. Many birds depend on people to leave food for them.

▶ City birds flock to the squares where they search for food. Many birds know that people will feed them. These birds have little fear of people.

▼ A swallow's nest in the roof of a building. This European swallow will fly 6,875 miles to southern Africa just before the winter comes.

Birds on Islands

▼ Guillemots and razorbills crowd on to the rocky cliffs of an island in the Atlantic Ocean. No food is available on the island. All the birds catch fish from the sea.

Islands are areas of land surrounded by water. Some islands are very small, while other islands are hundreds of miles wide. All islands can be divided into two main types. The islands which are close to land, or the **mainland**, are called offshore islands. Other islands found far out to sea are called oceanic islands. Most birds and other animals can reach offshore islands. The oceanic islands are difficult for most animals to reach. Birds can reach the bleakest and loneliest of islands.

Most oceanic islands are formed when **volcanoes** appear from under the ocean. These islands are just bare rock when they are first formed. The plants and the animals arrive over a long period of time. Some are carried on to the islands by the wind, while others float to the islands.

Birds are some of the first animals to arrive on these islands. Many types of animals never reach oceanic islands.

Nesting Sites

Both types of islands are visited by the seabirds. These birds use the islands only as nesting sites. They find their food in the sea. The offshore islands are used because most egg eating animals live on the mainland. The seabirds nest in huge colonies on these safe islands. Sometimes whole cliffs become white from their droppings. The oceanic islands are also very important to the seabirds. They may be the only nesting sites for thousands of miles around. They are also safe places to nest because the only predators are some other types of seabirds.

New Types of Birds

Flocks of small birds are sometimes blown to oceanic islands by chance. Usually, small birds would not cross the huge oceans. The first birds to reach an oceanic island are very lucky because they do not have to share their food with other birds. If a small flock arrives, some may begin to eat the seeds. Others may prefer to eat the insects. The beaks of these birds will change shape over thousands of years as they adapt to the environment. The birds become different types, or **species**. This has happened on many Pacific islands.

The islands of Hawaii once contained 22 types of honey creepers. Some of these have become extinct. Scientists believe that all the honey creepers came from one type of bird. The Galapagos islands have 13 types of finches. All these finches came from one type of finch.

Some birds are found only on islands. The Caribbean islands each have their own type of hummingbird. The kiwi birds of New Zealand and the palm chats of Hispaniola have no close relatives.

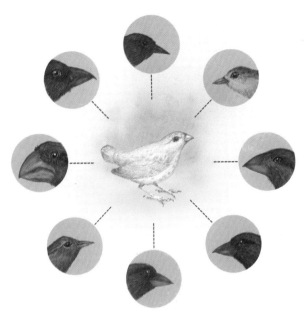

▲ The beaks of some of the types of Galapagos finches. Each beak is shaped to eat certain foods. These types of finches are found only on the Galapagos Islands.

▼ The kiwi is a rare, flightless bird. It lives in the swampy forests and woodlands of New Zealand. Kiwis are active at night when they look for worms and young insects.

Birds in Danger

There are almost 80 types of birds which have died out or become extinct over the last 200 years. This number is larger than any other animal group. Most of these birds lived on islands; many of them were flightless birds.

Some 350 types of bird are close to dying out today. These are **endangered** birds. Some types of birds have only 20 pairs left. Other types have as many as 1,000 pairs.

What Kills Birds?

Birds become endangered for many reasons. Some are at risk because other animals kill them or take their food. Most birds are endangered because of people.

Many island birds are endangered because people now live on their islands.

The dodo was a type of bird which died out when people came to its island habitat and killed them for food. People brought animals which ate the dodo's eggs and the young. The birds of New Zealand, like the kakapo, have also suffered when people have introduced new birds and animals to the islands. These animals have eaten the plants which the island birds used for their food and shelter.

People have changed the face of the earth. We have cut down the forests and the woods. These areas and the marshlands have been turned into farmland. Much of the habitat for the birds has been destroyed. Some birds are killed by **chemicals** which are used on farm crops. A chemical called DDT has killed many birds of prey. DDT weakens the shells of their eggs. This means that the chicks die before they are ready to hatch. Most countries no longer use this chemical.

▼ The flightless kakapo is a type of parrot. This rare bird is found in a few valleys of New Zealand.

▲ The imperial eagle was once common in Spain. Fewer than 100 survive today.

▼ The dodo became extinct 300 years ago. It had no defense against people and animals.

How Birds Can Be Saved

The best way to save the birds is to stop the destruction of their habitats. Many more birds will die out if the forests and the marshes are made into farmland or used for industry. Some countries have set up safe places, or **reserves**, for the birds. Also, some countries have passed laws to protect rare bird types. These laws stop people from catching the birds or stealing their eggs. Many birds of prey have been saved by these laws.

The rarest birds can be saved by breeding them in zoos. The numbers of Hawaiian goose, the California condor, and the whooping crane have been increased in this way.

We have learned many lessons from the past. Some of the birds, like the dodo, and the passenger pigeon could have been saved. People today are learning to be more careful and to protect birds in danger.

Glossary

adapt: to change in order to survive in different surroundings.

air sac: an air-filled "balloon" found inside a bird's body. Birds have many air sacs. The air sacs are part of a bird's breathing system.

albumen: the colorless fluid which makes up the white of an egg. Albumen becomes solid when it is boiled.

amphibian: an animal which begins its life in water, but lives on land when it is adult. Frogs, toads, newts, and salamanders are amphibians.

ancestor: a relative that died a long time ago.

backbone: a line of bones found inside the backs of birds, fish, amphibians, reptiles, and mammals.

bark: the outer covering of tree trunks and branches. Some trees have rough, thick bark. Others have smooth, thin bark.

bird of prey: a bird which kills and eats other animals. The birds of prey include the eagles, hawks, and buzzards.

breastbone: a strong, light bone down the middle of the breast to which the ribs and muscles are attached. In flying birds, the breastbone is large and surrounded by muscles which flap the wings.

breed: to produce young.

brood: all the young birds which are hatched from eggs laid about the same time.

camouflage: the color patterns or body shapes which help to hide an animal's body in its surroundings.

canopy: the top layer or "roof" of a forest. The canopy is formed by the treetops touching one another.

chemical: any substance which can change when joined or mixed with another substance.

chick: a young bird. Chicks can run around soon after hatching from the egg.

colony: a large number of birds which live together in the same area.

coniferous forest: a type of forest made up of trees called conifers. Coniferous trees have cones and keep their leaves all through the year. Pines, firs, and spruces are examples of conifers.

courtship: the type of behavior which male and female animals carry out before they mate.

courtship dance: a series of actions which a bird performs to attract a mate.

crag: a high, sharp rock.

crop: a "bag" in the throat of some birds. The crop is used to store food which is passed to the stomach later.

dinosaur: one of a group of reptiles which died out 65 million years ago.

display: an act which a male bird performs to scare away other males. Male birds also display to "show off" to and to attract females.

down: a fine, soft type of feather which grows next to a bird's skin.

drag: the force which slows an object down as it flies through the air.

eave: the edge of a roof which hangs over the walls of a building.

endangered: describes any type of animal or plant which is in danger of dying out. Many endangered animals have become extinct because of people.

Equator: the imaginary circle which goes around the middle of the earth. The Equator divides the northern part of the earth from the southern part.

experiment: a test which is carried out to discover something which is unknown.

family: a group of animals of a similar type.

feather: one of the coverings which grows out of the skin of a bird.

filter: to separate a solid object from a liquid or air.

fledgling: a young bird which is old enough to leave the nest, but cannot fly or feed itself yet.

fossil: the remains of an animal or plant, usually found in rocks. A fossil can be the bones of an animal or the shape left by the animal's body in the rock.

glide: to move through the air without power. A bird does not flap its wings when it is gliding.

graze: to feed on grass.

grub: a young insect.

habit: the usual way in which an animal behaves.

habitat: the place where an animal usually lives.

incubation: the act of sitting on eggs in order to keep them warm before they hatch.

intruder: an unwanted and often unfriendly visitor.

keratin: the hard material which birds' feathers are made of. Hair, reptiles' scales, and human fingernails are also made of keratin.

lift: a force which raises an object into the air.

lung: a part, inside the body, of an animal which is used for breathing air. All birds have lungs.

mainland: a large area of land. A mainland may have islands off its coasts.

mammal: an animal with a warm body which is usually covered in fur. Mammals give birth to live young which feed on the mother's milk.

marrow: the soft material which is found inside the bones of many animals.

marsh: a piece of low-lying land which is usually wet.

migrant: an animal which makes a long journey at certain times of the year.

migration: the movement of animals over long distances to find food, to produce young, or to escape from cold weather.

molt: to lose old feathers, fur, or skin. Birds do not molt all of their feathers at one time.

nectar: a sugary liquid which plants produce in their flowers.

nestling: a young bird which is helpless when it hatches from the egg.

order: the scientific name for a group of animals.

oxygen: a gas found in the air. All animals must breathe in oxygen to live.

pair: a male and a female bird which build a nest together in order to produce young.

perching bird: the common name for the largest group of birds. Most perching birds are small. They have feet which are shaped for clinging to twigs or for perching on branches.

plumage: all the feathers of a bird.

polar region: either of the parts of the world which are found close to the South Pole or the North Pole.

prairie: a large, open area of grassland.

predator: an animal which lives by hunting and eating other animals.

preening: the cleaning, oiling, and smoothing of feathers.

pterosaur: a type of flying reptile which died out 65 million years ago.

reptile: a member of a group of animals which includes snakes, lizards, crocodiles, and turtles. All reptiles have dry, scaly skins and lay eggs with shells. Reptiles cannot make their own body heat.

reserve: a special area of land in which wild animals can live in safety.

savanna: a hot, dry grassland with few trees.

scavenger: an animal which feeds on decayed food or on the dead bodies of other animals.

scrape: a simple "nest" made on the ground. Scrapes use very little nest material.

season: one of the four periods of time during the year. The seasons are spring, summer, autumn and winter. Each season has a certain type of weather.

skeleton: the hard part of an animal's body which gives it support and shape. All birds have a bony skeleton inside their bodies.

soar: to glide and rise into the air without effort. A bird soars by riding on a current of air which is rising.

soaring bird: a bird which flies high up into the air without having to flap its wings.

species: a particular type of animal or plant. Animals of the same species look alike and can breed with one another.

streamlined: shaped in a way that it can move through the air or water as easily as possible.

talon: one of the sharp, hooked claws on the foot of a bird of prey.

territory: the area of land lived in and guarded by a bird. Birds guard their territories to make sure that they have enough room to feed and to produce young.

thermal: a hot, rising air current.

thrust: the force which moves an object forward. A bird's wing produces thrust to move the bird through the air.

tropical rain forest: a type of forest found in the hot, wet parts of the world close to the Equator.

vertebrate: an animal with a bony skeleton and backbone. Fish, amphibians, reptiles, birds, and mammals are all vertebrates.

volcano: a type of mountain. Volcanoes are formed when very hot liquid is forced up from deep inside the earth. As the liquid cools it leaves a mountain of rock.

wader: a type of bird with long legs which feeds in shallow water. Most waders have long, thin beaks. Waders include snipe, curlews, and sandpipers.

warm-blooded: describes an animal which can keep its body at a steady temperature. It does this by making its own heat. A warm-blooded animal can also lose heat if it gets too hot.

waterproof: anything that is made so that water cannot pass through it.

weave: to cross leaves or stalks over and under each other to form a large, single piece of material.

webbed feet: describes the type of feet that many water birds have. Webbed feet have a layer of skin between the toes. This helps the animal to paddle through the water.

yolk: the yellow, central part of an egg. The yolk contains food for the developing young bird.

Index

air sac 10
albatross 25
albumen 17
amphibian 4
Antarctic bird 22
Archaeopteryx 7
Arctic bird 23
Arctic loon 26
Arctic tern 20
auk 23

barbet 33
bird
  beak 11, 26, 32
  breastbone 7, 12
  breathing 10
  breeding 14, 20
  camouflage 11, 18, 30
  colony 42
  crop 31
  egg 16, 17
  endangered 44
  feather 4, 11, 24, 36
  flight 12
  fossil 7
  nest 11, 16, 17, 28, 29
  plumage 8, 28
  senses 10
  skeleton 4, 10
bird of paradise 15, 33
bird of passage 20
bird of prey 9, 10, 19, 33, 36, 37, 38, 45
booby 24
bowerbird 32
broadbill 16, 33
bullfinch 35
buzzard 37

capercaillie 36
chaffinch 35
chick 18
chickadee 19
chough 39
cock-of-the-rock 32

condor 38
  California 19, 45
cotinga 32, 33
courser 30, 31
courtship 15
courtship dance 32
crane 26
  common 20
  whooping 45
crocodile 6
crossbill 36
crow 5, 35
curlew 26

desert wheatear 31
dinosaur 6
dipper 27
display 14, 15
diver 26
  black-throated 26
dodo 44
down 5
duck 20, 23, 26
  canvasback 26
  mallard 26
  teal 26
  tufted 26

eagle 9, 13, 14, 36, 38
  golden 38
  harpy 33
  monkey 33
egg 16, 17
egg tooth 18
Emperor penguin 23
emu 9, 29

falcon 9, 36, 40, 41
  peregrine 37
finch 31, 35, 43
flamingo 9
fledgling 19
flight 12
flycatcher 34, 35
fossil 7
frigate bird 15, 24

gannet 24, 25
goldfinch 35

goose 20, 23, 26
  blue 20
  brant 20
  graylag 20
  Hawaiian 45
  snow 20
goshawk 37
grebe 15, 26
grouse 28, 36
  willow 23
guillemot 17, 24, 25
gull 9, 22, 23, 24, 25, 40

hawfinch 35
hawk 9, 36
heron 26
honey creeper 43
hornbill 16, 33
hummingbird 9, 33, 43
  fairy 8

Ichthyornis 7
incubation 17

jay 35

kakapo 44
keratin 11
kingfisher 9, 27
kiwi 43

lammergeier 38
lark 28
lyrebird 32

magpie 35
mammal 4, 5
manakin 33
martin 40
migrant 20, 34
migration 20, 21, 34
motmot 33
mourning dove 31

nest 11, 16, 17, 28, 29
nestling 18, 19
nutcracker 36

ostrich 8, 29
ovenbird 16, 28
  red 28
owl 36, 37
  burrowing 28
  eagle 37
  horned 37
  snowy 37

palm chat 43
parrot 33
peacock 15, 32
penguin 5, 9, 22, 23, 24
perching bird 9, 38, 39
petrel 22, 24
pigeon 40, 41
pitta 32
plover 26
  Egyptian 31
  golden 20
plumage 8, 28
prairie chicken 28
pratincole 31
ptarmigan 23
pterosaur 6

razorbill 24
reptile 4
rhea 29
roadrunner 30, 31

sanderling 20
sand grouse 31
sandpiper 26
scrape 28, 29
seabird 19, 24, 25, 42
sheathbill 24
skeleton 4, 10
skimmer 24
skua 23
snipe 26
soaring bird 13
sparrow 40, 41
sparrow hawk 37
starling 40, 41
stork 26
summer visitor 20
sunbird 16
swallow 16, 20, 40, 41
  bank 20
swan 26
  whooper 20
swift 19, 40, 41
  chimney 40

tanager 33
tern 20, 23, 24, 25
territory 14, 15
thermal 13
thrush 40
  ground 32
tit 19
toucan 33

tree creeper 35
tree-lizard 7
tropic bird 24
turkey 9

umbrella bird 15

vireo 35
  red-eyed 20
vulture 9, 13, 38
  bearded 38

wader 26
wading bird 20, 23, 26
wall creeper 39
warbler 34, 35
weaver bird 16
wetland bird 26, 27
winter visitor 20
woodpecker 9, 11, 35
  acorn 35
wren 14

yolk 17